The Truth At Last!

a Discourse on Generated Reality

George Arthur Lareau

(Sufi George)

SUFI GEORGE BOOKS
TUCSON

The Truth at Last!

ISBN 978-1-885570-20-8
Library of Congress Control Number: 2010910332

SUFI GEORGE BOOKS
TUCSON
http://sgbooks.sufigeorge.net

Dedicated to You

I dedicate this book to you, the young people who were born and live in our time of rapid and turbulent change.

This little book is an orientation guide to current reality.

My wish is that it will end your confusion and empower your life.

With best wishes,

Sufi George

The Truth at Last!

Contents

Permit Me to Introduce Myself 7
I Find Nothingness 11
I Find Lucid Dreaming...12
The Truth at Last! 14
Do you believe in frequency waves?.....................17
We Get Frequency waves 18
The New Paradigm View 20
The Ice Cream Demonstration 22
Common Sense Gets Dumped................................24
Which Truth Are You Going To Follow? 26
Slaves to Empire Builders 27
The Common Universe 29
Your True Self..30
Our Purpose In Life..33
Beta, Theta and Delta Realities 34
The Spaces Between Wavebands..........................37
Frequency Wave Behaviors 40
The Dalai Lama's Take..41
The DMC...45
The Mind 48
Our Status as Teammates 50
How We Began 51
We Are Smart People 53
But We're Not Enlightened 54
My Sufi George Books 57

Three Peaks 57
**Sufi George's Coloring Book of Consciousness
Management Study Aids**..58
Mind Blow, Understanding Consciousness.........58
Create Reality with Morphic Robots 59
Sufi George Comix 59
Some Interesting Links...60

Permit Me to Introduce Myself

I'm speaking to you as a minister, because, well, I am a minister. I hesitate because I've spent very little of my lifetime in churches. That's because of the way I was called to the ministry.

As a child, I found refuge in church from my abusive home. I was in the choir loft from age 10. I was president of everything. At age 14, at summer church camp, I suddenly saw a clear image of myself on the clear blue sky. I was at a pulpit, and—here's the catch—truth was flowing through me.

I saw and felt myself preaching truth. Not religion, but truth.

At first, I thought that the truth was what the church taught me. They had big buildings so they must know the truth, I figured.

Then at another summer church camp I was ambushed by an evangelist and got saved by the ever-flowing blood of Jesus, and my truth changed. This truth was all printed out on little cards that you memorize. It made preaching easy.

After a year or so of this truth, I asked questions for which there were no cards. The answer was faith, just believe, just take it on faith. I tried that for a while, but it nagged at me.

When I considered that people around the world have faith in very different beliefs, I doubted that faith was enough. I needed to set a higher standard.

I suffered when I dumped my faith-based beliefs. It not only left me bereft of truth, it destroyed my career path. I set myself to the task of finding out the actual truth behind the nature of consciousness and reality.

It was my junior year of college, and I almost flunked out because I spent almost all of my time in the library, reading anything and everything that might give me a clue; you know, starting from scratch and all, where do I begin?

I chose to pursue the big picture, explanations of the universe itself. My first important find was Theosophy which laid it all out including pretty illustrations and the names of the gods. I took this idea with me to Boston where I joined the beatniks.

I met Larry Davis who was a follower of Kirpal Singh, an Indian guru, and I checked this out for two years and finally went for it because it offered proof. It was just another faith-based belief, one of the thousand paths to truth. I had meditated two hours daily for fifteen years, following a vegetarian diet, with only moderate results.

I read another 5000 books during this time and still found a thousand paths leading to one goal. And it's not that any path will work, it's that the paths are all fighting with each other, so none of them ever gets anywhere near the goal. They're all mired down in their particular beliefs and superstitions.

The guru wasn't all wrong. But he was just one of thousands who pick up the thread that there is such a thing as alternate reality. That's where the neat stuff happens. And they weave that thread into the fabric of their mythology.

I have been a Reverend since age 16, when the Methodist church granted me my preacher's license. I served one year as assistant minister at a Methodist church in Belleville, IL. But the more I chased after truth, the farther away I got from the church.

I Find Nothingness

Finally, around age 40, after having served my Buddhist family phase, I read **The Tao of Physics** by Fritjof Capra. This book gave me scientific explanations that applied to my metaphysical questions. Everything jelled, suddenly. I read the book twelve more times; I had never studied physics before.

During meditation I flew out of my body starting at my feet. I flew out of the top of my head, through the starry universe, and ended up in nothing at all. I was aware of myself. And I was aware that I was in a vast black expanse made of shimmering dots but the shimmering was black also. Everything had disappeared and there was no sound, no light, no time, and only myself for company. I didn't think at all, not in thoughts. I became aware that I was examining the black dots, rather than having decided to look at them.

Since that experience, I have felt no fear. I have repeatedly recreated my life with detachment as if watching a movie. I have no fear of death. Nothing is as serious as it used to be.

I Find Lucid Dreaming

Anyway, my next important discovery was lucid dreaming, how to be awake and aware while asleep and dreaming. This is a scientific doorway to alternate reality. I was between wives at the time so I devoted myself to learning lucid dreaming. Within a few weeks, I was having great results. Lucid dreams are much more exciting than Disneyland or any other ordinary reality.

Several scientific discoveries that seem at first too abstract to care about are actually keystones to a view of reality that is very different from what we think we know.

When I found that I had scientific discoveries to work with, I swore off belief once and for all. Except for believing in science. Joining the work of other writers, I wrote a new paradigm theory of the universe and of consciousness. My unique contribution is my Dynamic Model of Consciousness.

Do I finally know the truth? Can I preach now? I've been waiting for the day when the truth I trust answers my burning questions, and in such a delightful way. It is an emerging truth so there's no sense in waiting for everything to finish. It doesn't finish. So I will preach now, starting at age almost 70.

The truth I recognize is not mine alone. Many people are getting the new paradigm message across. There are numerous books, lecturers, movies, etc. I am one of those; I am a preacher.

Now about the truth. At last.

The Truth at Last!

New paradigm means a new way of thinking, a new perspective or view of things. Today's new paradigm revolves around scientific discoveries that completely upset our common knowledge. Our knowledge of reality is changing around us and we have to catch up with it.

Our common sense about reality is totally and completely wrong. There is no material reality; it's a matrix of frequency waves, similar to the movie. There is no material at all until a contact with consciousness stimulates subatomic particles to assemble from chaos into the pattern we are looking for. Looking for something can make it manifest. This is particle physics.

Such truth greatly increases our opportunities for living our lives in new ways. First, it lifts a huge culturally-induced burden of guilt and fear by letting us break away from past myths and live in trustworthy truth. This is a great liberation.

Second, it greatly increases our ability to recreate and manage our reality. Hundreds of books discuss the power of the mind, but today's science shows us the interactions of frequency waves that generate our experience of reality.

We all have the ability to create, and when the obstacles are removed, we are free to actually do it.

I may have raised a few questions in your mind. I suppose you are in some shock at learning that the universe is nonmaterial and so are you. You may fear that you will suddenly dissolve into the patterns of frequency waves that you are made of like those people who spontaneously combust.

Do you believe in frequency waves?

Do you believe in frequency waves? They are invisible, nonmaterial patterns flying through space. And if you believe that one, well, it can't be helped. Science has shown us that this invisible, nonmaterial pattern is a very useful reality.

Here's a simple experiment. Look at a thing. Two hundred years ago, the thing could only be made of matter. This experiment suggests another option. You can see the thing because some of the light waves that are bouncing off it are going into your eyes. Two hundred years ago you couldn't have known this because you didn't know about frequency waves.

Close your eyes and the thing disappears. Two hundred years ago, the thing was still there even though you couldn't see it. This experiment suggests another option. Open your eyes and the thing reassembles itself from chaos. That is, it reappears.

So let's demonstrate this.

We Get Frequency waves

Light waves are frequency waves, of course. These waves travel into your eyes and are stopped by the retina. From there, their data are interpreted by your consciousness system which assembles it into an experience that you can see and feel. But this all happens in your consciousness, in the dark, not out there. Close your eyes and consciousness stops producing the video. The thing goes out of existence.

The way we experience this depends on whether or not we know about frequency waves. Without that knowledge, the thing can only be out there. With knowledge, we see that it's really a virtual reality created in our consciousness, the matrix.

Now, no one in history would understand or believe any of this. But in our times, we use frequency waves in hundreds of ways, so if we think that frequency waves aren't real, we're just lying to ourselves. We can't help knowing better.

Okay, so light waves go in our eyes, sound waves go in our ears, etc., and out of that complex package of wave patterns, we get the picture. We experience life. But it is not experience that gives us life. We have life first, even when we close our eyes. Life is the ability to experience. It's our consciousness, our awareness in particular.

This means that life is what we choose to look at. Awareness itself is empty until we pay attention to something. And then our awareness experiences it. We can manage our attention. It's the one thing we can do, the one power we have for generating our reality.

The New Paradigm View

With this understanding of reality, the new paradigm view of reality, our lives open up to us. We become self-managers instead of victims. We diminish our egos, our set of fabricated personalities, keeping them under observation and management; that is, our egos lose control, leaving us free to use them creatively to manage our lives.

With our understanding of frequency waves, we know the answer to that old riddle: If a tree falls in the forest and there is no one to hear it, does it make a sound? We know that the answer is: there are only silent sound waves, and there is no sound until the waves reach consciousness, at which point someone hears the sound, inside their consciousness.

This of course greatly disturbs our common sense experience of reality. But based on our knowledge of frequency waves, we know first-hand that this new paradigm view of reality is true.

As this realization sinks in, we increasingly back-step away from this illusion of reality, pulling our attention away from its magnetism, and orienting ourselves as the observer of our lives as well as the actor.

When this shift in the focus of our attention is substantial, we can begin to witness our intentions generating our reality.

The Ice Cream Demonstration

I was teaching this to one of my private classes and to demonstrate I created ice cream. Well, nothing happened immediately, but after the class as we lingered talking outside the door, my landlady walked up with two ice cream cones. She said, I got one for my husband but he didn't want it. This had never happened before.

Common sense says that this is an example of coincidence. But I see the interactions of fields of frequency waves. I estimate that she had just enough time to get the ice cream cones if she started when she received the impulse that I had sent out in all directions.

I had no idea how the ice cream would be generated. I didn't want this little demonstration to fail in front of my students. And I love ice cream.

I wasn't worried about it as we stood talking. I was answering questions and wasn't even thinking about it at that time. And then it just happened, surprising us all. Managed generations of reality always surprise me because they are usually cute and clever in the way they arrange their manifestations.

Larger scale generations take more work but are equally possible. Solving major problems, for example, make it necessary to dissolve obstacle patterns. This is done by depriving them of our attention, and that takes practice in focusing on the positive instead.

Major problems consume a great deal of our attention. We find ourselves paying a lot of attention to our dire circumstances and their doomy consequences. But remember, we experience what we pay attention to. Paying attention to the problem feeds the problem because it keeps it connected with our awareness, the energy of the universe.

When you close your eyes, your generated reality disappears. When you open them, pay attention to what you can now create, what reality you can now generate, not on the problem. This takes some practice but anyone can do it, and when they can, opportunities are everywhere and problems are a video game.

Common Sense Gets Dumped

I suppose your common sense is in a state of shock. You are perhaps knocking on the wall to see if it is real. The fact is, you have no choice in the matter. You know the truth.

Yes, it turns your common sense on its head, but that's what is happening to people these days. Yes, it leaves you gasping for air, feeling helpless and alone, until your perspective flips over from the ancient delusion to the new paradigm reality.

This is an evolutionary stage for us. Two hundred years ago this wasn't possible for humans except for a very few. We are making a leap into a reality that is both abstract and material, where we watch and manage their interplay.

Very well, that doesn't seem to quell your common sense qualms. You may be wondering how you could have been so completely wrong about everything for your whole life. In fact, you probably don't believe it for a minute because like all of us, you are so in love with being right.

Which Truth Are You Going To Follow?

The question is this: Which truth are you going to follow? Let's look at the truth you have now.

Your common sense truth is all second-hand, truth that came at you from outside of yourself. Your family, your community, your culture all have fed you the truth you now have and believe is right. And if you had been born in a different part of the world, it would be all different.

Look at where this truth came from. Where did your parents get their truth, the truth they passed on to you? From their parents? How many generations back does this go? How out-dated is this truth today? Where did this truth originate? Who created it? Was it the empire builders? Are you in fact enslaved by the truth of the builders?

Slaves to Empire Builders

As long as the masses believe the illusion of generated reality, empire builders are able to manipulate their truth. Masses of believers in anything are first of all believers, and their beliefs can be shaped because beliefs are not based on first-hand knowledge.

Your truth was designed to make you a slave to empire builders. This is the way things have always been. If you are satisfied living such a life instead of being liberated from all that and free to create your life as you wish, common sense will work for you.

Your common sense truth should now be an embarrassment to you. New paradigm truth may destroy a lot of your reality, but when the cocoon opens, you will be able to fly.

Look at the stars at night. They are all contained in your consciousness, ancient light waves entering your eyes. The entire universe exists within you. This is only possible because you have awareness, the first thing ever. Close your eyes and the universe disappears. That is, your universe disappears.

The universe disappears because it is no longer in contact with your awareness, the only place where it can be real. Until and unless the wave patterns that you see as the universe pass through awareness, they are just patterns, abstract, invisible patterns wandering around as inventory.

My universe doesn't disappear just because yours does, though. This means that each of us has a universe to himself. Who could ask for anything more?

Now, how did we get to that conclusion? We each own our own version of the universe and nobody can take it away from us. We are compelled to reach that conclusion because we know about frequency waves.

But why then does my universe look so much like yours?

The Common Universe

We are all cooperating on some level to keep our common universe going. We are all working together to maintain our common material reality, simply by paying attention to it. So the sun never sets on the universe.

Our common universe provides us with a shell to get born into. It is a ready-made universe in which we can explore possibilities and opportunities. As we explore, we add our experience to the shell and the shell grows.

The Truth at Last!

In our personal universe, we have freedom subject to the constraints of the common universe. We can make a wide range of choices in our lives. We can see our choices generate in reality.

We have creative energy. We can think and we can make things. It is a power we have. We create our experiential lives with this power.

Your True Self

At some point soon, find liberation from your experiential lives and recognize your generic nature. After that, life goes on but the seriousness is toned down.

Also, your true self shows you that you are not the life you are living but the person watching your life being lived. Your true self has a view of your life as an elaborate theatre production, and your true self is playing director for this life.

The most interesting thing about the true self is that it is not material. Some say that consciousness is created by the brain, without realizing that conscious awareness must necessarily be there first, and that it generates the brain as a material reality.

Our nonmaterial true self does not die. The material body dies because awareness loses contact with the vital wave fields. We become disconnected from the body. Game over.

The rest of our personal universe is still there. It's just the body problem, no sensory input. Otherwise, we're good.

The common universe is still there. You could travel or ghost around or whatever. The point is, there's plenty to do without a body.

Or you could find a new entry point and do it again.

Doing it again is what it's all about. We are all part of the group that began the universe and we've been developing it ever since. Each of us has played many parts many times in this endeavor, each time contributing something to the common universe.

We may or may not choose our birth circumstances but either way it's sink or swim after that. Every set of circumstances imposes limitations on our choices no matter what, and we must see what we can do within our individual limitations.

We do bring everything with us, however. Stored somewhere are our memories of past lives. And depending on what's in our bag, that can be an advantage. We can call on the abilities and talents within us and continue to develop them. That's how one gets to be a Mozart.

For now we are mostly oblivious to these memories. They are all history now and we're moving on. But our talents and abilities shine through.

Our Purpose In Life

Our purpose in this life is to make one more contribution to this common universe of ours. We are punching in for work on our project. That project includes ourselves and the world around us.

Look around to see what contributions people are making to the common reality. We see everything from philanthropists to throw-away trash.

If only people could somehow know their purpose. Our common universe would kick into hypergrowth. Everyone would be enlightened and empowered and would look for positive choices.

Everything that happens is the result of our choices. We experience what we pay attention to. We can choose what we pay attention to. Paying attention is a choice.

When we pay attention to something, we are (literally) tuning in to its frequencies. Our consciousness system decodes those frequency wave signals and we experience that something. When we choose to pay attention to something else our experience changes.

Beta, Theta and Delta Realities

Experience is the life we are living. In the material world, our attention tunes in to patterns in this particular waveband. We call this Beta reality, named after the brain wave patterns we emit when we're tuned in to this waveband.

When we sleep and dream, our Beta reality vanishes and we experience dream reality, called Theta reality. And all that has happened in this shift from Beta to Theta reality is that our attention has tuned in to a different waveband.

Frequency waves enter our consciousness system where they are decoded into experiences, whether we're in Beta reality or in Theta reality.

Our Beta mind, the logic system in us that interprets Beta reality into such vivid detail, is mostly asleep when our attention is tuned into Theta. The mind we use in Theta is different so we interpret things with very little logic and less vividness.

The Truth at Last!

The dividing lines between different wavebands are spaces where there is nothing to pay attention to. The attention is thus free to wander into other wavebands.

Ideally, we would have our Beta mind fully awake while we are tuned in to Theta reality. Then we could experience the freedom of the dream world with all of our mental faculties intact. We can use the freedom to experience anything we can think up.

This state is called Delta reality, and we can access it by learning lucid dreaming. It is a reality that is extremely vivid and makes us hate to wake up. Recommended are the books on lucid dreaming by Stephen LaBerge of Stanford University.

In comparison to a place like Delta reality to retreat to every night, the turmoil of Beta reality will seem to play out like a game. Beta reality's common universe is no longer the only option for experiencing life, and that takes a load of pressure off.

Many people use lucid dreaming to sort out their Beta reality problems and arrive at creative solutions. Where you can do anything, why not do that? Learning lucid dreaming is a choice that you can make. So, will you?

The fourth waveband is Alpha, and most people know this one. It is for imagination and daydreaming, essentially a creative environment. It is also a stress reducer which is reflected in its slower brain waves.

The Spaces Between Wavebands

Those spaces between wavebands...there is nothing there. Unfortunately, we are unaware of this emptiness. Our attention drifts through it without sending us any signals. We would experience nothingness if only our attention would focus on our awareness itself.

Unfortunate, I say, because the consciously aware experience of nothingness is enlightenment. It shows us what remains when all reality disappears, when experience stops. There is only our awareness and the awareness that we exist.

There is only that true self, awareness plus the self that is aware, a self delimited by an attention function. We see our true selves in purity when we focus our attention on our awareness and on nothing else.

Every one of us is the same. We just tune in to different frequency wavebands within the common universe.

Without attention to narrow our experience to specific wavebands, we would be aware of everything at once, a state of chaos.

Similarly, our Beta reality lives may be chaotic because our attention is spread over too many wavebands, what we call overload.

New paradigm reality turns our view of the world upside-down. It is so radically different from anything we've ever considered. But now that we have the knowledge, can we turn our backs on the fact that we know about frequency waves? It all begins and ends with frequency waves. We are lost in the matrix until we understand this.

Everything I've said has science behind it. The scientific knowledge is available; just switch your TV to the science channels. Or read some of the hundreds of books that are available.

This presumes, however, that you respect science as a source of truth. If you find your truth in some system based on blind faith, it may teach you to reject science.

Truth is anything you believe it to be. It is your personal universe and you are free to accept any truth you choose to believe. If you change your beliefs, you change your truth.

In the end, it doesn't really matter what you accept as true. The only absolute truth is the reality of awareness, and all other truth is relative. It's just that it's a shame to reject a truth system that is liberating, enriching, enlightening and that comes from the best efforts of our most dedicated smart people.

Frequency Wave Behaviors

Frequency waves have specific behaviors. Understanding these sheds a lot of light on our experiences in Beta reality when we can visualize how frequency wave patterns are created and how they interact. We can make and watch them happen.

Dan Russell of Kettering University has done a wonderful job of animating frequency wave behaviors. It's on the web: search for _Acoustics and Vibration Animations_.

These basic patterns operate on each level that is made of them, with each level becoming increasingly complex and becoming things like people, but retaining the same set of basic behavior patterns.

The Dalai Lama's Take

Here's how the Dalai Lama describes what we are calling the new paradigm experience of life:

Dalai Lama: ...it is quite difficult to have an experience of Dzogchen, but once you do have that experience, it can be extremely beneficial in dealing with your day to day life, your job, and your career. This is because that kind of experience will give you the ability to prevent yourself from being overwhelmed by circumstances, good or bad. You will not fall into extreme states of mind: you will not get over-excited or depressed. Your attitude toward circumstances and events will be as if you were someone observing the mind, without being drawn away by circumstances.

For example, when you see a reflection of a form in a mirror, the reflection appears within the mirror but it is not projected from within. In the same way, when you confront the situations of life, or deal with others, your attitude too will be mirror-like.

Also, when a reflection appears in the mirror, the mirror does not have to go after the object that is reflected: it simply reflects, spontaneously, on the surface. The same with you: since there is no attachment or agitation at having these 'reflections' in your mind, you will feel tremendous ease and relief. You are not preoccupied by what arises in the mind, nor does it cause you any distress. You are free from conceptuality or any form of objectifying. And so it really does help you, in allowing you to be free from being caught up in the play of emotions like hatred, attachment, and the like.

--from *Dzogchen: The Heart Essence of the Great Perfection*

Mystics have long taught this message in the context of many different cultures. The culture of science makes it finally crystal clear, without the clutter of antiquated cultural artifacts.

This knowledge is powerful. Learning and understanding it changes everything for you. It is freely available to you and to everyone. It can be simply chosen and you are on your way. So, will you?

Search for popular books on quantum reality, particle physics, cosmic consciousness, etc. My own books present my specialization, creation of a visual Dynamic Model of Consciousness (DMC).

The DMC

I always wanted to know how consciousness actually works, the dynamics of it, and it took me 40 years to get it. I illustrate its components and actions in the DMC.

In the DMC, awareness is represented as a dot at the center of a model that looks a little like Saturn. Surrounding awareness is a clear crystal ball kind of field through which frequency wave patterns, from any direction, must pass before they reach awareness.

Eccentrically orbiting around this is a small ball representing attention. Travelling at tremendous speed, its orbital pattern looks like a ring around intuition, like the rings of Saturn.

The three components of consciousness are awareness, intuition and attention. We have control only over attention.

Attention tunes in to something. Those frequency waves resonate with attention because attention resonates with awareness, connecting through intuition.

So the frequency waves pass through attention, then pass through intuition which because of its lens-like qualities as a crystal ball magnifies the size of the waves, and on they go into awareness for the actual experience.

Then they pass out through intuition again which decreases their size.

But they no longer continue in a straight line. They have a resonant connection to the pattern that is you and this traps them in an orbit just like gravity would.

We can remember experiences. For that to happen, those patterns have to travel through attention, intuition and awareness again.

Remembering an experience calls that pattern back into the center of the DMC, via resonance. The pattern emerges out the other side of intuition and loops back through the center of awareness and forms an infinity shaped course which it continues to travel, trapped in our experience infinity loops.

These experience loops remain with us forever. None of our experiences is ever lost. We can remember past life experiences if we tune our attention to them.

The DMC illustrates how paying attention to specific frequency waves brings them into our experience and preserves them in our memory.

Intuition in the DMC isn't everything we usually think but it is the part of the consciousness system where patterns can enter awareness without first passing through attention, that is, without us thinking about them first.

These signals are always from a different waveband and can come from any direction as long as they don't pass through attention. They feel impulsive because they bypassed our mind.

The Mind

The mind, that busy machine that interprets the incoming signals into patterns that we can recognize as experience, this mind of ours is a fairly recent evolutionary development. That is, our group couldn't create the mind until everything else was in place.

In the DMC, the mind is a small ball that orbits the ball of attention. Attention routes the signals it receives to mind and mind spins them back to attention in processed form.

Mind learns its rules for interpreting reality from the experiences that pass through it. You can blame your experiences for being the mess you are. (But whether you remember it or not, they were all choices you made by paying attention to them.)

Education gives our minds a breadth of new experience, and study trains our attention to focus where we choose. With an educated mind and new possibilities to explore, we can recreate our lives by controlled attention alone, plus, of course, seizing our opportunities when they present themselves.

An educated mind always questions truth systems, realizing that there is only one absolute truth, the reality of awareness, realizing that we are all working together to advance the truth of our common universe.

Our Status as Teammates

We are working for a universal truth that everyone can understand and respect. When this transition completes, people will abandon their faith-based belief systems and agree on the generic nature of all people. Our relationships will be cooperative, contributing, each in our own way, to the continued building of our common universe.

When we understand that each of us is a consciousness system made of awareness, the basic stuff of the universe, and that we are equally empowered to contribute something to the common universe, we can stop hating and fighting.

When we understand that we have all been teammates on this project from the very beginning, we can be cooperative. Everyone in the world is on the team plus many who are on sabbatical.

We still have a lot of work to do on our common universe, and we'll probably want to see just how far we can take it. But still, we've come a long way, baby.

How We Began

First, there was awareness. Awareness became aware of itself, and that is an experience, and this experience multiplied mathematically, creating an infinite chaotic ocean of frequency wave patterns within awareness, not even waves yet, just the nonmaterial patterns, they were numbers actually, and that's where we come from.

We organized ourselves into attention so we could deal with the chaos bit by bit. We divided attention into bits because each bit could work independently. We were amazing. As bits.

We all created something, anything, just to get the techniques down. Later, we agreed on a project that would enable us to experience a continuous reality, that is, to live in time where things continue their existence. And, we wanted to experience living in 3D space, our coolest concept.

That was the beginning of the common universe, and after a long time we as humans are now waking up to the realization that it's our baby. We are not only responsible for taking care of it, we are responsible for creating it from scratch, and for continuing the project.

We Are Smart People

And I think that makes us pretty smart people. Just look at what we've built so far. We've even extended outer space. But look at Earth, our garden delight where some of us worked on creating the birds and others the trees.

We are a brotherhood of universe creators. It's okay to develop our personal universes and that way contribute to the common universe. It's not okay to force our personal universe on someone else.

Worse, it's not okay to force one's personal universe on the common universe itself, to try to take over the world.

Any positive contribution to our common universe results from cooperation, not from force.

But We're Not Enlightened

We seem to have a problem with this. Wars. We fight over our faith-based beliefs in value systems. The solution to wars is not in winning them. It is in correcting the disconnect we have from our true selves.

Our true selves have strong relationships with each other. We have worked together side by side for eons. We have huge families. Forgetting this enables our killing mode. We feel alone because we are disconnected. We kill our own, our friends, our relatives, our lovers.

It's pure disconnect. If governments want to stop war, they could try the completely different strategy of educating people about new paradigm reality.

This is the time of enlightenment. Necessarily so, because it's the only way we have left to save our planet, our garden. Can the outcome be predicted?

We have the help of legions of us who are working on our common reality while they are between lifetimes. The enlightenment will occur. It is our tool of last resort.

We've worked too hard and long on the Earth and we don't want to lose it now. The enlightenment will put an end to many projects underway and cause a lot of change, but no regrets, mate.

Your part in this begins in your personal universe. Become one of the enlightened yourself. It is necessary to do this first because only you can choose it and only you can do it.

The Truth at Last!

I've given you enough information and leads to just go ahead and get started. You can find a lot of help on the web and in books and films. Git 'er done and then educate someone. Let's save ourselves and our planet.

With best wishes,

Sufi George

My Sufi George Books

http://sgbooks.sufigeorge.net

Three Peaks

This is my first Sufi George book. I had to establish my standards for truth before I could develop any further. Three Peaks is a careful analysis of the four pathways that bring truth to us. I'd like to rewrite this book sometime because the style is cumbersome, but meanwhile this edition gets the information across.

Sufi George's Coloring Book of Consciousness Management Study Aids

This is a meditative exercise that results in wall charts on identity, truth, and consciousness. The book was hand-made and is now out of print. The text of the book and directions for wall charts are included in **Create Reality With Morphic Robots.**

Mind Blow, Understanding Consciousness

My second book, this is a collection of articles written in the Sufi George altered state of attention. I describe the Dynamic Model of Consciousness, and provide several mind exercises.

Create Reality with Morphic Robots

My third book, I present my complete awareness theory of consciousness and the universe. Using this, I show how to create morphic robots, mental wavefield creations that manifest as our Beta realities.

Sufi George Comix

This comic book, filthy, rotten and certainly depraved humor, is my parody of Sufi George. First, check out new paradigm reality. If you do that, you will see through my filth filter and get the "Sufi-like" messages in the comics. I think they're funny. Some make me laugh until I fart.

Some Interesting Links

My Home Page:
http://sufigeorge.net/

My Shockwave animation of Sufi George's Dynamic Model of Consciousness:
http://sufigeorge.net/dmc270.swf

Sufi George Books on amazon.com:
http://sgbooks.sufigeorge.net

My Helpful Books & Films Suggestions:
http://astore.amazon.com/sufigeorgnewp-20

The Ascent of Humanity by Charles Eisenstein
http://www.ascentofhumanity.com/text.php

Bohm's Gnosis: The Implicate Order
http://www.bizcharts.com/stoa_del_sol/plenum/plenu
m_3.html The Cosmic Plenum:

Power of Thought - A Quantum Perspective - By Kent
Healy
http://www.youtube.com/watch?v=FeFuc-
qFKoA&feature=related

Kymatica
http://topdocumentaryfilms.com/kymatica/

Vibration creates matter
http://www.youtube.com/watch?v=2DGPV7SB88c&fe
ature=related

George Carlin - Religion is bullshit.
http://www.youtube.com/watch?v=MeSSwKffj9o

Bill Maher lays waste to Religion
http://www.youtube.com/watch?v=qYW2xXxFVtU&fea
ture=PlayList&p=F3D646A0AF403BC0&playnext_fro
m=PL&playnext=1&index=40

Richard Dawkins - "What if you're wrong?"
http://www.youtube.com/watch?v=6mmskXXetcg&feat
ure=PlayList&p=3EC216E8B93349C2&playnext_from
=PL&index=19&playnext=2

Best of Bill Maher on Religion
http://www.youtube.com/watch?v=WmUvhKr9SPk&fe
ature=PlayList&p=B630ACFBA4EBDF7D&playnext_fr
om=PL&index=0&playnext=1

Best of Bill Maher on Religion (Continued Fun!)

The Truth at Last!

http://www.youtube.com/watch?v=ZuoBPGvXFAs&feature=PlayList&p=B630ACFBA4EBDF7D&playnext_from=PL&playnext=1&index=1

Bill Maher Be More Cynical on religion
http://www.youtube.com/watch?v=4FZeHvJDxas&feature=PlayList&p=B630ACFBA4EBDF7D&playnext_from=PL&playnext=1&index=2

John Hagelin, PhD on Consciousness 1 of 2
 http://www.youtube.com/watch?v=OrcWntw9juM

Amit Goswami, Quantum Physics & Consciousness 1 of 3
http://www.youtube.com/watch?v=s42mrdhKwRA

www.ingramcontent.com/pod-product-compliance
Lightning Source LLC
Chambersburg PA
CBHW021223020426
42331CB00003B/438